HIGHLIGHTS FROM THE HUBBLE TELESCOPE
Postcards from Space

Melanie Chrismer

Series Advisors:
Marianne J. Dyson
Former NASA Flight Controller
and
Gregory L. Vogt, Ed. D.
NASA Aerospace Educational Specialist

Enslow Publishers, Inc.

40 Industrial Road	PO Box 38
Box 398	Aldershot
Berkeley Heights, NJ 07922	Hants GU12 6BP
USA	UK

http://www.enslow.com

Library of Congress Cataloging-in-Publication Data

Chrismer, Melanie.
    Highlights from the Hubble telescope: postcards from space / Melanie Chrismer.
        p. cm. — (Countdown to space)
    Summary: Details the initiation of the Hubble Space Telescope in
April 1990 and the repair and servicing missions which followed, and
explains the telescope's role in answering questions about the universe.
    Includes bibliographical references and index.
    ISBN 0-7660-2135-1 (hardcover)
    1. Hubble Space Telescope (Spacecraft)—Juvenile literature. 2. Outer
space—Exploration—Juvenile literature. [1. Hubble Space Telescope (Spacecraft) 2. Outer
space—Exploration.] I. Title. II. Series.
QB500.268.C485 2003
522'.29—dc21

                                                                2002152434

Printed in the United States of America

10 9 8 7 6 5 4 3 2 1

To Our Readers: We have done our best to make sure all Internet Addresses in this book were
active and appropriate when we went to press. However, the author and the publisher have no
control over and assume no liability for the material available on those Internet sites or on
other Web sites they may link to. Any comments or suggestions can be sent by e-mail to
comments@enslow.com or to the address on the back cover.

Photo Credits: Bruce Balick (University of Washington) and NASA, p. 4 (Twin Jet Nebula);
Dr. Christopher Burrows, ESA/STScI, and NASA, p. 31; Jeff Hester and Paul Scowen (Arizona
State University)/NASA, p. 29; Erich Karkoschka (University of Arizona) and NASA, p. 20 (c);
Jon Morse (University of Colorado) and NASA, p. 4 (Eta Carinae); NASA, pp. 13, 14, 41;
NASA, John Bahcall (Institute for Advanced Study, Princeton), Mike Disney (University of
Wales), p. 39; NASA, ESA, and J. Clarke (University of Michigan), p. 19; NASA, ESA, and K.
Sahu (STScI), p. 30; NASA and L. Esposito (University of Colorado), p. 16 (right); NASA, A.
Fruchter and the ERO Team (STScI, ST-ECF), pp. 38, 42; NASA, J.P. Harrington and K. J.
Borkowski (University of Maryland), p. 27; NASA and The Hubble Heritage Team
(STScI/AURA), pp. 4 (Reflection Nebula, Little Ghost Nebula, Galaxy ESO 510-G13, Ant
Nebula, Hoag's Object, Spirograph Nebula, Whirlpool Galaxy M51), 7, 17 (Jupiter), 20 (a, b),
28, 34, 37; NASA, P. James, Steve Lee, and Todd Clancy, p. 16 (left); NASA, NOAO, and STScI,
p. 35; NASA, Robert O'Dell, and Kerry P. Handron, p. 26; NASA and A. Riess (STScI), p. 6;
NASA and John Spencer (Lowell Observatory), p. 4 (Io); NASA, Donald Walter (South
Carolina State University), Paul Scowen and Brian Moore (Arizona State University), p. 23; Dr.
H. A. Weaver and T. E. Smith (STScI), NASA, p. 17 (comet pieces); Brad Whitmore (STScI) and
NASA, p. 11.

Cover Photos: NASA, H. Ford (STScI), The ACS Science Team, and ESA (foreground);
Raghvendra Sahai and John Trauger (JPL), the WFPC2 Science Team, NASA, and AURA/STScI
(background).

*Cover Photos: Hubble's Advanced Camera for Surveys was installed during the fourth servicing
mission in 2002. The first four images released to the public were (clockwise, from top right) the Cone
Nebula, a pair of galaxies called The Mice, the Omega Nebula, and the Tadpole Galaxy.*

CONTENTS

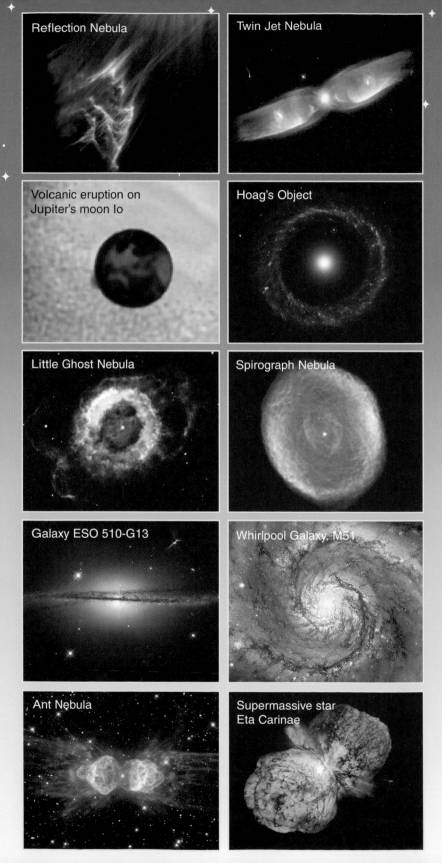

Reflection Nebula

Twin Jet Nebula

Volcanic eruption on Jupiter's moon Io

Hoag's Object

Little Ghost Nebula

Spirograph Nebula

Galaxy ESO 510-G13

Whirlpool Galaxy, M51

Ant Nebula

Supermassive star Eta Carinae

1

Seeing Is Believing

"The past ten days have been an unbelievable experience," said Dr. Robert Williams, formerly of the Space Telescope Science Institute in Baltimore, Maryland.[1] For ten days in December 1995, the Earth-orbiting Hubble Space Telescope had its camera aimed at a familiar part of the sky. The camera snapped over three hundred photos of a tiny piece of the star pattern Ursa Major. This constellation includes the Big Dipper. But the pictures were not taken of the bright stars. Instead the telescope was looking at a tiny area between the stars that looks empty to the naked eye.

The pictures revealed one of the greatest discoveries made with the help of the Hubble Space Telescope. The photographs show tiny, colorful wavy lines and

In 1995, the Hubble Space Telescope focused on a tiny region of the sky for ten days. The photos showed more than 1,500 galaxies! The tiny region of the sky is called Hubble Deep Field.

dots—minute representations of more than 1,500 star-packed galaxies.

A galaxy is a gigantic group of millions, or even billions, of stars. A galaxy is so large that its size is measured in light-years, and some are thousands of light-years across. A light-year is the distance light travels in one year, almost 6 trillion miles (9.6 trillion kilometers).

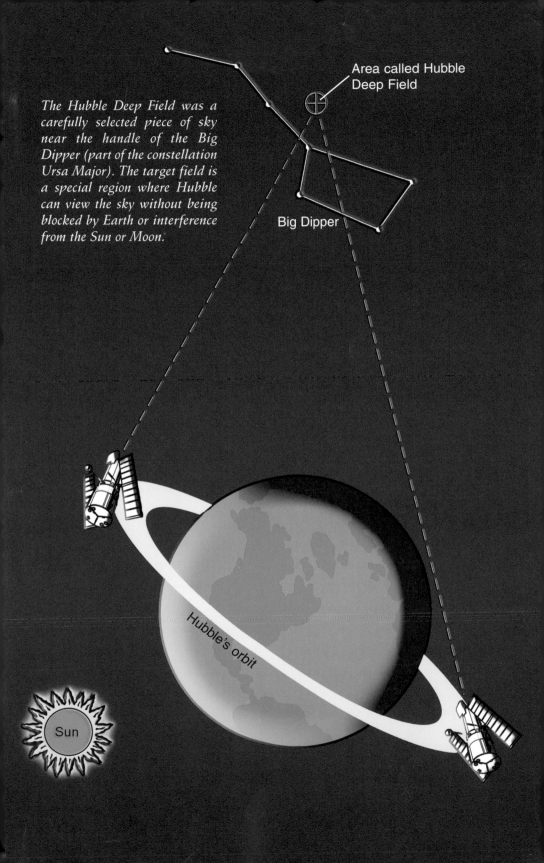

Area called Hubble
Deep Field

The Hubble Deep Field was a
carefully selected piece of sky
near the handle of the Big
Dipper (part of the constellation
Ursa Major). The target field is
a special region where Hubble
can view the sky without being
blocked by Earth or interference
from the Sun or Moon.

Big Dipper

Hubble's orbit

Sun

The new galaxies spotted by the Hubble Deep Field Project in December 1995 were billions of light-years away. This means that the light coming from most of these galaxies took 10 to 12 billion years to reach Earth.[2] Scientists wonder whether these new images reveal the first lights to shine in the universe.[3] If so, the universe could be at least 12 billion years old.

The area where these galaxies exist looks very small from Earth. Imagine looking at the night sky through the eye of a needle held at arm's length. All the new galaxies, quasars, and supernovas that the Hubble photographed at that time would appear to fit inside the needle's eye.

Harry Ferguson, another astronomer on the Hubble team, judged the group's findings like this: "One of the great legacies of the Hubble Telescope will be these images."[4]

Hubble has allowed scientists to look deeper into outer space than anyone had ever looked before.[5] The same piece of sky when viewed through a ground-based telescope might not show anything at all. But when viewed using the Hubble, the black sky reveals galactic details never seen before.

With the discoveries from the Hubble Space Telescope, people on Earth are seeing more and more details of space. But there is still a vast universe out there waiting to be seen. Science is asking questions. Hubble is helping with the answers.

2

What Makes the Hubble Special?

Looking into the night, early astronomers could only see dots of light on a black dome-shaped sky. Around 1609, Italian scientist Galileo Galilei started using a telescope to study the sky. This new tool led to some amazing discoveries, such as that Jupiter had moons. Galileo was able to study the other planets in our solar system. His observations helped prove that the Sun was at the center of these planets.

As larger telescopes were made, the knowledge of what lay beyond our planet Earth also grew. The more scientists learned, the more they wanted to know. Earthbound telescopes continued to improve through the twentieth century, but they faced one major obstacle: Earth's atmosphere prevented a clear view.

The atmosphere is like a blanket of gases that protects Earth from dangerous radiation, meteorites, and extreme temperatures. Unfortunately, it also gives astronomers a fuzzy view of space. The gases that surround Earth prevent even powerful telescopes from getting a completely clear look at the universe.

Hubble to the Rescue

In 1923, an astronomer named Hermann Oberth suggested placing a telescope in orbit above the atmosphere.[1] It took sixty-seven years to make it happen, but in 1990 the Hubble Space Telescope was ready to be deployed. This telescope was named for astronomer Edwin Hubble in honor of his discovery that the Milky Way was not the only galaxy.

Hubble was first launched into space in April 1990 aboard the space shuttle *Discovery*. It was released from the shuttle into orbit around Earth. The scientific community was thrilled. But when images from the telescope were relayed to Earth, scientists discovered that one of its mirrors had not been made correctly. Because of this problem, special corrective optics were developed. Like a nearsighted person getting glasses, Hubble could see much better. After four space shuttle servicing missions, the Hubble's observations are clearer than when it was first designed.

Usually, the bigger the telescope, the sharper the images. Hubble is not as big as some of the ground-based

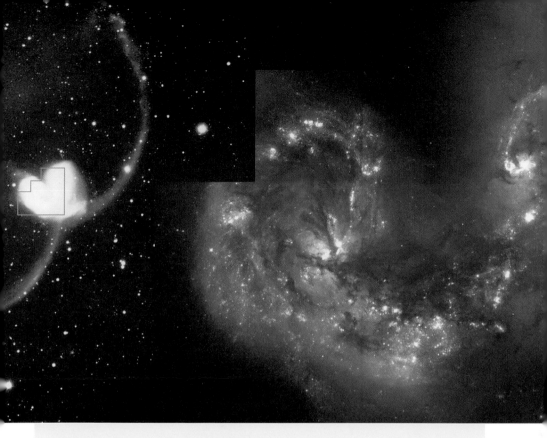

The image on the left shows the Antennae galaxies as seen by a ground-based telescope. The image on the right shows the same galaxies, as seen by the Hubble Space Telescope. The two orange blobs are the cores of the two colliding galaxies.

telescopes, but the images are from above the atmosphere (that's the secret), so Hubble's images are the sharpest. This orbiting telescope was not designed to replace ground-based telescopes, such as those at the Mount Palomar and W. M. Keck observatories. Ground-based telescopes have a wider view than Hubble does, and they cost much less to build. (Compare Hubble's initial cost of over $1.5 billion to the $140 million price tag of the Keck Observatory, which houses two ground-based telescopes.) On the other hand, Hubble can see much farther into space—even beyond our galaxy. Scientists often use Hubble together with ground telescopes. For example, a ground-based telescope might find something in the sky for Hubble to investigate closer. Images from the Hubble and other telescopes can be laid over one another for comparison.

How Does the Hubble Work?

Orbiting Earth every ninety-seven minutes, the Hubble is a reflecting telescope with two mirrors. It is about the size of a tractor-trailer. The light comes in through a long tubular opening. This light is reflected by the two mirrors and eventually onto scientific instruments such as the Wide Field Planetary Camera 2 (called WFPC2) and the Near-Infrared Camera and Multi-Object Spectrometer (called NICMOS). These instruments allow special and unique views of space. The information travels by satellites from Hubble to the Space Telescope Science Institute, and then on to other scientists.[2]

Along with these instruments, the Hubble has equipment that no other ground telescope has. For example, it gets its energy from the Sun through two power-generating solar panels. These panels charge Hubble's batteries for use in Earth's shadows.

The most exciting thing about this telescope is the new view of the universe it gives to people on Earth. Hubble's discoveries are analyzed by scientists who plan, research, and study the pictures and data captured by this unique telescope. Scientists and mathematicians estimate that there are billions of galaxies to study.

Dr. Fritz Benedict, an astronomer at McDonald Observatory in Texas, says, "I am honored to practice astronomy using the Hubble Space Telescope. Because of this telescope, our abilities have increased about the same huge amount as when Galileo put the first telescope into the service of astronomy. Before Hubble Space Telescope, the work I do was nearly impossible."[3]

With each servicing mission, the Hubble Space Telescope has been improved. In March 2002, two astronauts performed a spacewalk. Their job continued the mission that gave Hubble a better camera, a recharged spectrograph, an improved power pack, and brand new solar arrays.

Hubble Space Telescope

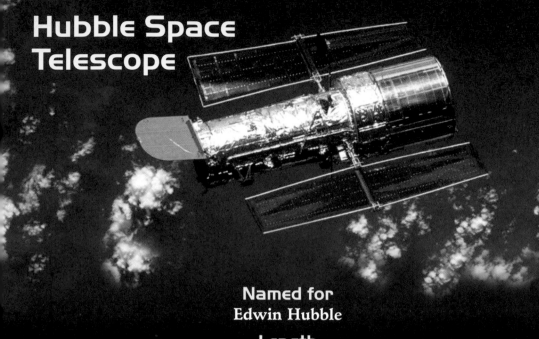

Named for
Edwin Hubble

Length
43.5 feet (13.2 meters); about the size of a bus

Weight
12 tons (11 metric tons); about the weight of six minivans

Launched
April 24, 1990, on space shuttle mission STS-31

Released into orbit
April 25, 1990

Orbit
Approximately 380 miles (612 kilometers) above Earth
It takes about 97 minutes for each orbit.

Speed
17,500 miles per hour (28,000 kilometers per hour)

Size of telescope
14 feet (4.2 meters) in diameter

Size of mirrors
Primary mirror is 7.9 feet (2.4 meters) wide
Secondary mirror is 1 foot (30 centimeters) wide

Control Center
Space Telescope Science Institute
Baltimore, Maryland

3

Looking at the Backyard: The Solar System

The Hubble Space Telescope doesn't just see into deep space. It also looks at Earth's backyard—objects in our own solar system. The solar system includes the Sun, nine planets, asteroids, and comets. Photographs of the solar system are some of the highlights from the Hubble's first ten years in orbit.

The Closest Neighbors

Hubble provides scientists with new details about Venus. In January 1995, Hubble looked at Venus 70 million miles (113 million kilometers) away. It photographed the planet and collected data with a spectrograph, a tool that separates light waves into colors and lines. Hubble scientists used this data to find out what gases make up Venus's atmosphere. Now they knew for sure that the clouds above Venus are made of sulfuric acid rather than water vapor.

The Hubble has been viewing Mars carefully and has taken photographs of changing Martian weather. Hubble even showed a planet-wide storm. Astronomers want to know more about the pink sky, ten-mile-high dust storms, and freezing clouds. Views of the Martian poles give a full-color look at ice caps surrounded by rusty red sand.

In 2001, Hubble snapped an image showing a huge dust storm as it swept across the surface of Mars.[1] New photographs lead to new questions to answer about Mars. Hubble helps provide the answers.

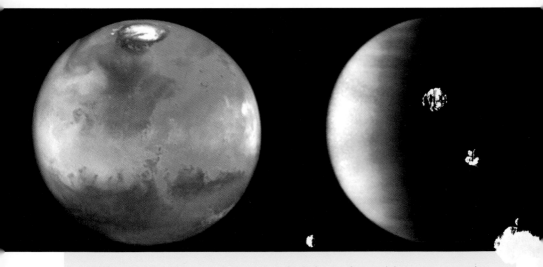

Although Hubble was designed to look beyond our solar system, it has supplied the most detailed pictures yet of Mars and Venus. Images of the northern ice cap on Mars (left) and the atmosphere of Venus (right) are just some of Hubble's highlights. The images inspire new studies by planet scientists.

For six days, pieces of the Shoemaker-Levy 9 Comet struck Jupiter. Hubble photographed the pieces of the comet, sometimes called "the string of pearls" (above). Hubble also captured the impacts (right), shown over time in the four photos of Jupiter. The dark areas appearing toward the bottom of the planet are the impact sites.

The Hubble has also been looking at the outer planets of the solar system: Jupiter, Saturn, Uranus, and Neptune. These planets are known as gas giants. They are not dense and rocky, but made of gas.

Comet Impacts Jupiter

For years, ground-based telescopes have watched Jupiter's gigantic storms. Jupiter's big red spot is really a big storm—like a hurricane bigger than Earth. In July 1994, mirrors were focused on Jupiter, but not for a storm. Exciting things were happening right in Earth's backyard that week, and Hubble was the lead photographer. The comet Shoemaker-Levy 9 was headed straight for Jupiter. Telescopes around the world spotted about twenty pieces of the comet stretched in a line. For seven days, the pieces collided with Jupiter's atmosphere. The comet pieces hit so fast that they vaporized, causing great plumes to form miles above the surface. Hubble captured these dramatic impacts. "I just didn't believe it was happening," said an amazed Dr. Rita Beebe of the Space Telescope Science Institute.[2] Hubble provided the best pictures to a thrilled science community.

Hubble Solar System Highlights

Although ground-based telescopes can see Jupiter's moons and Saturn's rings, the Hubble's specialized instruments can reveal these objects in greater detail. In 1998, Hubble photographed the glowing, swirling auroras at Saturn's north and south poles. An aurora is a spectacular light display in the upper atmosphere caused by strong magnetic forces at a planetary pole. In 2000, Hubble focused in on Jupiter's aurora at its north pole. The glowing gas circled the pole like a lasso. These auroral patterns are similar to the wavy glows of Earth's own auroras.

In 1994 Hubble took images of Uranus. Pictures studying its rotation, four major rings, seventeen moons, and clouds allowed the planet to be rediscovered in new details. Hubble's infrared camera clearly showed the rings, moons, clouds, and fierce storms of 900-mile-per-hour winds, and confirmed the tilt of the planet's axis. Uranus and Pluto are the only planets in the solar system with an extreme tilt. Earth and the other planets rotate

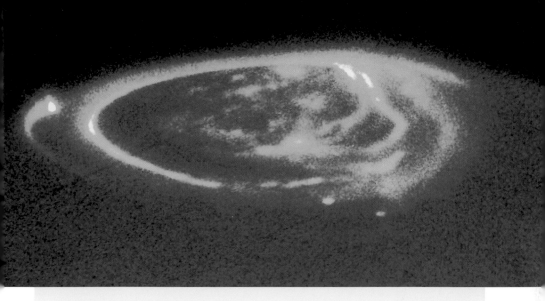

Hubble captured this magnificent image of the glowing aurora at Jupiter's north pole in 2000.

nearly the way a basketball spins on your finger. When compared to their path around the Sun, they are upright, or nearly so. But Uranus rotates as if it were rolling through its orbit on its equator. Thanks to the Hubble, astronomers could now be sure that views of Uranus from Earth showed its south pole or north pole facing us, and not the planet's equator.

Pluto is the farthest planet from the Sun and the smallest in the solar system. It is so far away and so little is known about it that every look gives scientists more information. Mysterious Pluto was 3 billion miles (4.8 billion kilometers) from Earth when Hubble photographed it. Definite dark and light areas were visible. Although Pluto had been mapped before, Hubble's Faint Object Camera gave Pluto a photographic face; scientists could see more details than ever before.

a. Hubble clearly presents Saturn's most recognizable feature: its rings.
b. This is the clearest view yet of Pluto (left) and its moon, Charon.
c. This image from Hubble shows the four major rings around Uranus. It also shows ten of the moons that orbit the planet.

The Hubble Space Telescope took the first photograph of Pluto and its moon Charon as separate objects. Hubble's ability to observe things at this distance is even more powerful than someone in New York City being able to count the candles on a cake in San Francisco.

Largest Solar System Discovery Since Pluto

Pluto's orbit around Earth extends into an area called the Kuiper Belt. The Kuiper Belt is a region that contains many icy objects, including comets. In 2002, Hubble helped spot and measure the largest object in our solar system since the 1930 discovery of Pluto. The object, named Quaoar, is about 800 (1,300 kilometers) miles across, about half the size of Pluto.

Comet LINEAR Pops Its Lid

Hubble is watching other backyard objects such as comets, which are small icy objects that orbit the Sun. In 2000, the comet LINEAR gave astronomers an unexpected show. Focusing the Hubble Telescope on the comet, scientists watched a chunk of the comet's crust blow off. This outburst can be compared to a volcanic explosion, as it sent dust spewing into space. Scientists were happy when the Hubble later discovered a small group of mini-comets left behind from the comet's explosion. For the first time, they had a front-row seat for viewing the breakup of a comet's nucleus.

While Hubble has helped scientists discover many things about objects in our solar system, the mighty telescope has not stopped there. It searches beyond the solar system for mysterious galaxies and nebulas deeper in space.

4

Watching the Neighborhood: The Milky Way Galaxy

Our galaxy, the Milky Way, is about 100,000 light-years wide.[1] Called a spiral galaxy, it is disk-shaped with a bulge in the center. As its starry central bulge spins, it trails spiraling arms. In the Milky Way, about six thousand stars are visible to the unaided eye, but the telescopic view gives us an estimate of more than 100 billion stars.

People have been seeing star patterns since they started gazing at the night sky. These patterns, called constellations, were named in ancient times after animals, Greek heroes, and other legendary characters. The same constellations are used today to guide scientists in the study of our galaxy.

A galaxy is not only a collection of stars and planets. There is gas and dust in between the stars. Some of this gas and dust collect into clouds. Hubble can capture images of the gas regions, or nebulas, when they are lit up by nearby stars.

Types of Nebulas

The term *nebula* simply means "cloud" or "vapor." In ancient times, people located many nebulas in the sky.

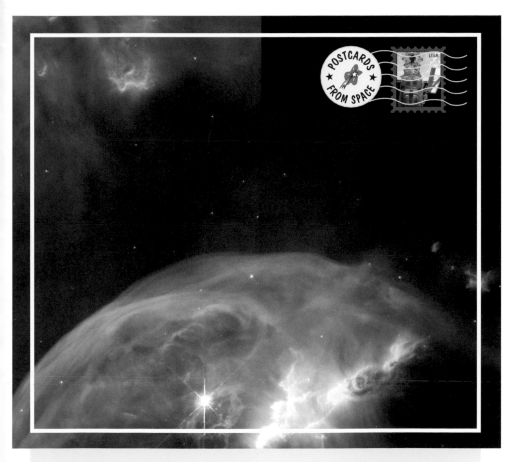

A nebula is the region of gas between stars. The Bubble Nebula, shown here, is located in the constellation Cassiopeia and is six light-years wide. Dense clumps of gas are located at the top of the picture. These fingers of molecular gas have not yet reached the expanding shell.

However, as humans have been able to focus their telescopes for clearer and clearer views of the sky, some of these cloudy objects have taken on definite shapes—they are not nebulas at all. Now *nebula* refers to gaseous regions between the stars, and the Hubble Space Telescope has given us our clearest pictures of them yet. Also Hubble's special filters and cameras can help scientists determine what fantastic combinations of elements are present in nebulas.

There are several kinds of nebulas. Reflection nebulas reflect light from nearby stars. Emission nebulas give off radiation from stars that are forming within them. This radiation makes the gases and dust in the nebula glow different colors. Hubble has shown us that emission nebulas are made up of mostly hydrogen. Dark nebulas absorb light, so they appear as dark clouds in the sky. Planetary nebulas are believed to be what is left of old stars after most of their energy has been used up. The remaining gas is usually helium, which expands and gets very hot until it glows. Supernovas are stars that have exploded. What's left after the explosion, a supernova remnant, is a nebula that can be a billion times brighter than our Sun. The Crab Nebula in the constellation Taurus is an example of a supernova remnant.

Orion Nebula

The constellation of Orion the Hunter is easily recognized by the ancient warrior's three-starred belt, his starry shoulders, and lighted limbs. On a clear winter's night, a fuzzy, almost green patch of light can be seen below Orion's belt. This is the Orion Nebula, an emission nebula. In the Orion Nebula, 1,500 light-years from Earth, bright new stars sit in a stellar nursery. The Hubble photographs it to help show the birth of stars.

Focusing in on the Orion Nebula, scientists believe they may be witnessing the beginning of a new solar system. Hubble's photographs of the Orion Nebula have allowed astronomers to discover protoplanetary disks within the nebula. Protoplanetary disks are areas in the nebula that may someday become new solar systems. The images of these disks are like nothing seen before: About half of the young stars in Orion are surrounded by disks.

Star Death

Just as stars are born, they also die. Pointing the Hubble in the direction of the constellation Aquarius, astronomers directed the telescope to photograph the Helix Nebula. At 450 light-years away, it is the closest nebula to Earth. It is a planetary nebula: It contains a star that is nearing the end of its life.

When a star dies, a series of changes leads to the collapse of its core. These changes can create colorful displays. Hubble's images of one section of this nebula reveal what look like yellow puffs shooting into the wind. These objects are called cometary knots, because they also look like comets. They have heads twice the size of our solar system and wispy tails that stretch 100 billion miles. The Hubble has found thousands of them in the Helix Nebula.[2]

Astronomers had seen the patterns made by the cometary knots before, but Hubble gave them a clear enough picture that they could finally figure out what caused them. Cometary knots are hot

The Helix Nebula is the closest nebula to Earth. It contains thousands of cometary knots, or comet-shaped new stars.

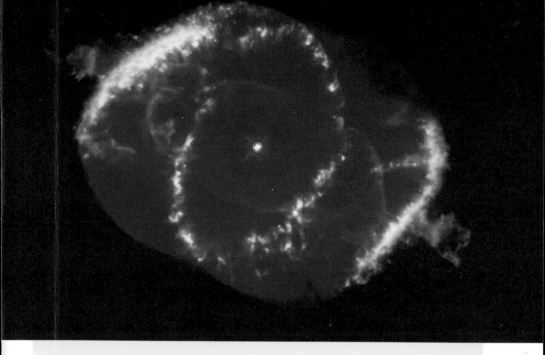

The Cat's Eye Nebula contains two stars at the ends of their lives, spewing their gaseous remains.

shells of gas spewed out by a dying star. When these shells pass over cooler (older) shells of gas, they break apart, trailing pieces in a long tail. Never before had scientists seen so many knots in a single nebula. It was another first for the Hubble Space Telescope.

More About Nebulas

Other images from the Hubble Space Telescope include those from the Cat's Eye Nebula.[3] This planetary nebula contains small stars at the ends of their lives. Rings of gas surround the stars. The fuel for the stars is used up. The collapse of the dying core is the last stage. Heat from the collapse makes the core very bright. The gas shells around it glow.[4]

There are young, middle-aged, and old stars in the Tarantula Nebula. A nearby star cluster (lower right) has several stars going supernova.

Hubble's photographs of stellar death are spectacular. In the Hubble's first full-color look at the Cat's Eye Nebula, it shows gas rings expanding out from two stars. It is a great picture of a star's farewell.[5]

Scanning for more Milky Way secrets, astronomers peek at the Tarantula Nebula. This nebula is filled with sheets and filaments of gas. Deep in the nebula, the birth of bright new stars is seen in fabulous Hubble pictures, revealed by its specialized instruments.

Eagle Nebula and EGGs

Hubble's instruments gave the world the most detailed look ever of the Eagle Nebula, another fascinating star-forming region.[6] The photograph is one of Hubble's best-known images.   Cloudlike

These dark pillarlike structures are actually columns of cool gas and dust that are also incubators for new stars. They are part of the Eagle Nebula.

Ground-based telescopes can see star clusters (inset), but locating individual stars in them can be hard. Not so for Hubble! This photo shows how Hubble can pinpoint the stars inside a cluster.

columns, called elephant trunks, appear in this emission nebula, which is 6,500 light-years away.[7] The shapes are visible through backyard telescopes, but when Hubble looks at them, it captures more than a fuzzy cloud. It sees towers of dust, glowing cold gas, and bright newborn stars. The newborn stars are hatching from globules, or pockets, of gas. The pockets are called Evaporating Gaseous Globules, or EGGs.

Young stars are forming in the dense gas of the columns. When the new star ignites, it gives off ultraviolet radiation. Hubble can see this ultraviolet light, so it can uncover the egglike globules of gas around the stars.[8] The dust-and-gas shapes, along with the new stars in the Eagle Nebula, give the scientific community exciting new details and examples of star formation.

One of the newest views the Hubble Space Telescope has brought to Earth is that of NGC 6093, a globular star cluster. It is a massive grouping of hundreds of thousands of stars.[9] Current studies are proving that there are many of these star clusters right here in the Milky Way Galaxy. Another new find is a Stellar Dust Ring. Hubble photographs show a hula-hoop shape around a star and possibly an area in the rings where new planets are forming. Thanks to the Hubble Space Telescope, there is a way to see these wonders, and even more beyond this galaxy.

Spectacular Supernovas

Thanks to the ground-based telescopes and Hubble, scientists have a greater understanding of supernovas. A supernova is the enormous explosion of an entire star. When a star goes supernova, it produces so much light it

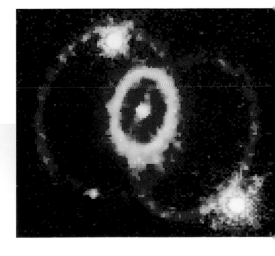

Supernova 1987A was discovered before the Hubble Telescope was launched. Since then, the Hubble has photographed the three rings of glowing gas encircling the supernova. The star exploded in February 1987.

may briefly outshine a galaxy as seen from Earth. It may even be visible without a telescope in the daytime. Some supernova leave a small, dense core behind.[10] Hubble sees these things better than any other telescope, observing changes in both visible and other wavelengths of light.

Before Hubble, in 1987, astronomers saw a star in the Large Magellanic Cloud explode, 169,000 light-years from Earth. Supernova 1987A, with its red-ringed, hourglass shape, is still being watched by Hubble's special equipment. Scraps from the supernova's core are expanding at 33 million miles per hour (53 million kilometers per hour). Dick McCray, a University of Colorado astronomer, is convinced that Supernova 1987A's remains will hit its outer rings very soon. Then, "We'll learn what that ring is. It's going to sparkle. . . ."[11]

Hubble is watching another star explosion inside the Milky Way. Eta Carinae is a giant variable star that is constantly changing its size and brightness (see photo on page 4). In 1841, Eta Carinae had a giant outburst. More than 150 years later, its cloud is still expanding. It looks like a supernova, but the star survived. Hubble data is helping scientists decide what happened.

5

Beyond the Milky Way: Exploring the Universe

The Milky Way is just one galaxy in a universe of billions. The teamwork between ground-based telescopes and the Hubble Space Telescope allows scientists to explore these massive groupings of stars, planets, and other materials throughout the universe.

Andromeda, at 2.2 million light-years from Earth, is the closest spiral galaxy to the Milky Way. Most spiral galaxies have one definite center, or core. Hubble's cameras have explored Andromeda, which has over 300 billion stars. The images confirm what astronomers had long suspected—that Andromeda has a double core. Scientists speculate that another smaller galaxy is passing through and is being consumed by Andromeda. Astronomers have observed that a collision of two

galaxies can be like the crossing of two flocks of birds; it is not destructive to the birds, but some birds will end up with the other flock.[1]

The Hubble has also found other types of double galaxies, called polar-ring galaxies. NCG 4650A, at about 130 million light-years away, is one of only a hundred known of its type. This galaxy used to be two separate galaxies. They collided but now coexist; one galaxy spins up and down, the other spins crosswise.

While two galaxies can collide and coexist, the two galaxies that seem to have collided in Centaurus A have not fared as well. Hubble has shown Centaurus A, 11 million light-years from Earth, in greater detail than ever before. Hubble images superimposed

A polar-ring galaxy is two galaxies that are coexisting.

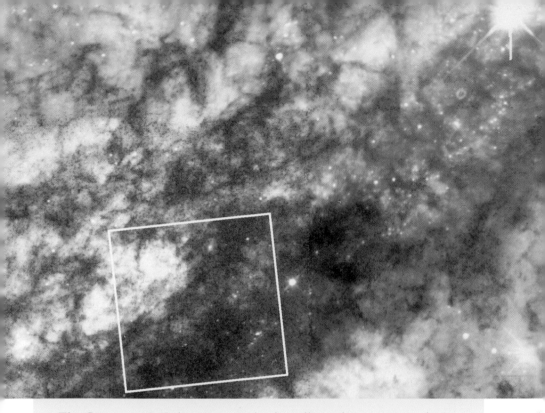

The Centaurus A Galaxy is a result of a collision between two galaxies. The box outlines an area where Hubble can see a gigantic spinning disk, larger than our Sun. It is trapped in the gravity of a black hole.

onto photos taken by ground telescopes show an oval galaxy filled with dust and gas. Dark areas in the galaxy are clouds of dust "finer than smoke," said Ray Villard of the Space Telescope Science Institute. There are glowing gas clouds, too.[2] The dust and gases seem to be the result of a galactic smash-up. Like the wreckage of a crash, collisions between two galaxies can result in a new object that does not look anything like either of the old galaxies.

Astronomers are studying Centaurus A to learn from the collision. When two spiral galaxies collide, a burst of star formation may follow. Hubble has captured images of groups and chains of brilliant blue star clusters around the edges of Centaurus A. Information from the Hubble gives astronomers a timetable for estimating when the collision occurred and how long it will continue. They think that, in the next billion years, the Milky Way Galaxy may collide with Andromeda in this same manner.[3]

Scientists can detect jets of particles shooting out of Centaurus A at nearly the speed of light and a disk that is spinning fast around *something*. Studies show a huge gravitational power, a sign of a black hole. Scientists think a supermassive black hole, 200 million times the mass of our Sun, is hidden within Centaurus A.

Discovering Black Holes

It is hard to investigate black holes because they cannot be seen. But like observing the wind bending a tree, scientists can see the effects of black holes on the gas around them. A black hole is formed when a massive star collapses. It has so much gravity that even light is sucked in and cannot escape. Black holes also suck in gas from nearby stars. Scientists use the Hubble to detect black holes because the telescope measures the velocity of stars, dust, and gas. Fast-moving particles whirling around inside a galaxy are evidence of a black hole. Depending on the speed of the gas, scientists can calculate the size of the black hole. While the Hubble gathers evidence of black holes, it also helps scientists

A black-hole powered jet of matter is traveling at nearly the speed of light. It is streaming out from the center of the galaxy M87.

count them. The information is being used to map each black hole's location.[4]

Even though black holes are invisible, a strong gravitational field makes it obvious that a supermassive black hole is right in the middle of the elliptical galaxy Virgo A (Galaxy M87), 50 million light-years from Earth. Virgo A contains a swirling disk of gas, and the galaxy itself spins at a tremendous speed in a whirlpool of gravity. The speed of the spinning indicates the size of the black hole, and this one is big.

Other galaxies are suspected to have supermassive black holes at their centers. Astronomers are using

A gravitational lens is the name for the event that shows images of stars and galaxies behind other objects with powerful gravity. The main objects in the image are 5 billion light-years away. The little blue marks are actually reflections of a target galaxy behind the starry cluster of galaxies.

Hubble research to hunt for evidence of these supermassive black holes. "The Hubble turned [theoretical black holes] into reality," said Ed Weiler, NASA's Associate Administrator for Space Science.[5]

Deeper Than Ever Before

The deeper Hubble looks into space, the more galaxies it finds. The Hubble Deep Field study continues to see the farthest parts of space yet. In March 2002, the space shuttle servicing mission again upgraded the Hubble

Space Telescope. Now Hubble has a view twice as large and ten times sharper than before.

The distance that can now be seen is approximately 12 billion light-years from Earth. This has increased by about 6 billion light-years since Hubble first looked past the stars of Ursa Major. The Hubble Deep Field study shows young galaxies, but the light coming from them is so far away that it took billions of years to get here. So the Hubble Space Telescope acts like a space history filmstrip: It shows objects the way they looked before Earth existed.

Answering Quasar Questions

In deep space, the Hubble Space Telescope is also showing astronomers quasars, or quasi-stellar objects. Quasars are distant unique points of light. They seem faint to the human eye but dazzling in other light wavelengths. They are really so bright that some are as bright as several billion stars all balled into one. Quasars may be the early centers of galaxies, full of activity, powered by supermassive black holes.[6]

Quasars look like stars when ground-based telescopes observe them. But Hubble can see more, showing that quasars are actually billions of times brighter than stars.

6

Seeing the Future

One of the Hubble Space Telescope's greatest accomplishments may be the possibilities for future research and the technology that stems from each Hubble Space Telescope upgrading mission. By the end of Hubble's eleventh year, 390,000 pictures had been taken and over 15,000 different objects studied.[1] The Hubble Space Telescope is finding new and unique highlights of space.

Back on Earth, Hubble continues to help scientists break new ground. Blind people are now being given Braille images made from the Hubble photographs. Hubble's images of galaxies, light-years away, can now be appreciated by everyone.[2]

Hubble images are now presented in Braille.

After Hubble

Improvements are being scheduled to help Hubble last until 2010. Since its launch in April 1990, servicing missions have continued to advance the orbiting observatory. Between December 1993 and February 2002, four missions kept Hubble at its best.[3] The latest mission provided equipment for a detailed view many times better than before.[4] One more upgrade is planned for 2004. The Cosmic Origins Spectrograph will be Hubble's most sensitive instrument. The Wide Field Camera 3 will be a wide-angle camera able to view the universe in every color.[5]

Hubble has many good years left, but new ideas for a better orbiting telescope are being planned. The James Webb Space Telescope, named after James E. Webb, NASA's second administrator, will have at least a 20-foot (6.1-meter) primary mirror instead of the 8-foot (2.4-meter) mirror that Hubble has now.[6] Until then, the Hubble is in a class by itself.

Thanks to the Hubble Space Telescope, the view from above the atmosphere is great. Through the Hubble's highlights and discoveries the universe is being seen more clearly than ever before. With the help of the Hubble Space Telescope, the universe is sending Earth postcards from space—snapshots better than humans could have imagined. Imagine what hidden mysteries are still waiting to be revealed.

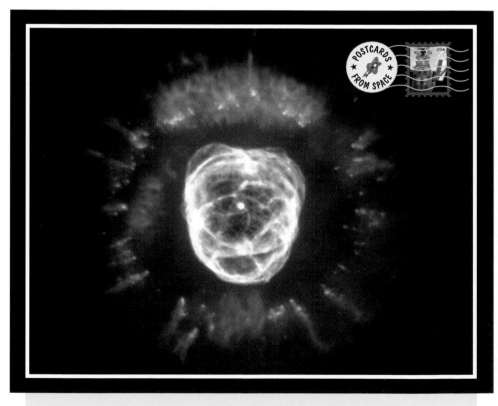

Hubble continues to take breath-taking images of space. More images, like this one of the Eskimo Nebula, can be expected until Hubble finishes its work in 2010.

CHAPTER·NOTES

Chapter 1. Seeing Is Believing

1. Robert Williams and Ray Villard, "Hubble's Deepest View of the Universe Unveils Bewildering Galaxies Across Billions of Years," January 15, 1996, <http://oposite.stsci.edu/pubinfo/press-releases/96-01.txt> (November 15, 2001).

2. Tom Wilkie and Mark Rosselli, *Visions of Heaven: The Mysteries of the Universe Revealed by the Hubble Space Telescope* (London: Hodder & Stoughton, 1998), pp. 160–165.

3. Williams and Villard.

4. Ibid.

5. Robert Williams, "Hubble's Deepest-Ever View of the Universe Unveils Myriad Galaxies Back to the Beginning of Time," January 15, 1996, <http://oposite.stsci.edu/pubinfo/captions/96-01a.txt> (November 13, 2001).

Chapter 2. What Makes the Hubble Special?

1. Wallace Tucker and Karen Tucker, *The Cosmic Inquirers: Modern Telescopes and Their Makers* (Cambridge, Mass.: Harvard University Press, 1986), p. 175.

2. Carolyn Collins Petersen and John C. Brandt, *Hubble Vision: Further Adventures with the Hubble Space Telescope*, Second Edition (Cambridge, U.K.: Cambridge University Press, 1998), pp. 14–16.

3. E-mail with Dr. Fritz Benedict, McDonald Observatory, University of Texas-Austin, September 27, 2002.

Chapter 3. Looking at the Backyard: The Solar System

1. Carolyn Collins Petersen and John C. Brandt, *Hubble Vision: Further Adventures with the Hubble Space Telescope*, Second Edition (Cambridge, U.K.: Cambridge University Press, 1998), pp. 34–38.

2. Interview with Ray Villard, Public Affairs Dept., Space Telescope Science Institute, at the STS-109 EVA press conference, March 5, 2002.

Chapter 4. Watching the Neighborhood:
The Milky Way Galaxy

1. Stuart Clark, *Universe in Focus: The Story of the Hubble Telescope* (New York: Barnes & Noble Books, 1997), p. 116.

2. Carolyn Collins Petersen and John C. Brandt, *Hubble Vision: Further Adventures with the Hubble Space Telescope*, Second Edition (Cambridge, U.K.: Cambridge University Press, 1998), pp. 74–78; 114–115.

3. Ibid., pp. 102–103.

4. Mark Voit, *Hubble Space Telescope: New Views of the Universe* (New York: Harry N. Abrams, Inc., 2000), p. 33.

5. J. P. Harrington and K. J. Borkowski, "Hubble Probes the Complex History of a Dying Star" *Planetary Nebula 6543* (Press Release No. STScI-PRC95-01), June 29, 1995, <http://oposite.stsci.edu/pubinfo/gif/NGC6543a.txt> (April 3, 2002).

6. Voit, p. 24.

7. Don Savage, Fred Brown, and Ray Villard, "Embryonic Stars Emerge From Interstellar Eggs" (Press Release No. STScI-PR95-44), November 9, 1995, <http://oposite.stsci.edu/pubinfo/press-releases/95-44.txt> (April 2, 2002).

8. Petersen and Brandt, pp. 78–79.

9. Ray Villard and Brad Smith, "Dust Ring Around Star Offers New Clues About Planet Formation" (Press Release No. STScI-PR99-03), January 8, 1999, <http://hubblesite.org/news_and_views/pr.cgi.1999+03b> (September 10, 2002).

10. Clark, p. 117.

11. Petersen and Brandt, p. 117.

Chapter 5. Beyond the Milky Way:
Exploring the Universe

1. Wallace Tucker and Karen Tucker, *The Cosmic Inquirers: Modern Telescopes and Their Makers* (Cambridge, Mass.: Harvard University Press, 1986), p. 167.

2. Phone interview with Ray Villard, Public Affairs, Space Telescope Science Institute, Baltimore, Maryland, November 20, 2001.

3. Terence Dickinson, *Night Watch: A Practical Guide to Viewing the Universe* (Willowdale, Ontario: Firefly Books, 1998), p. 94.

4. L. Ferrarese, "Dust Disk Around A Black Hole In Galaxy NGC 4261"/"Hubble Finds a New Black Hole—And Unexpected Mysteries" (Press Release No. STScI-PR95-47), December 4, 1995, <http://oposite.stsci.edu/pubinfo/gif/NGC4261C.txt> (April 5, 2002).

5. STS-109 Pre-flight Press Conference, National Aeronautics and Space Administration and Greenbelt, Md.: Goddard Space Flight Center video link, February 15, 2002.

6. Tucker and Tucker, p. 37.

Chapter 6. Seeing the Future

1. Bob Sillery, "The Facts: The Telescope," *Popular Science*, March 2002, pp. 79–80.

2. Ed Weiler, STS-109 Pre-flight Press Conference, National Aeronautics and Space Administration and Greenbelt, Md.: Goddard Space Flight Center video link, February 15, 2002.

3. Suzanne Kantra Kirschner and Michael Moyer, "What's New: Better Eyes for Hubble," *Popular Science*, February 2002, p. 11.

4. Nancy Neal, Goddard Space Flight Center, "Hubble Facts: The Advanced Camera for Surveys; Hubble's Powerful New Tool for Discovery," (Press Release FS-2002-1-035-GSFC), n.d.

5. Nancy Neal, Goddard Space Flight Center, "Hubble Facts: Hubble Space Telescope Servicing Mission 3B; Plans for the Future," (Press Release FS-2002—1-031-GSFC), n.d..

6. Phone interview with Ray Villard, Public Affairs, Space Telescope Science Institute, Baltimore, Maryland, November 20, 2001.

aurora—A glowing light display occurring near either of a planet's magnetic poles.

black hole—An object so dense that even light cannot escape its gravity.

comet—A small icy celestial object that orbits the Sun.

cometary knots—Glowing gas spewed out from a dying star.

elliptical—Having an oval shape.

galaxy—A large group of stars, planets, and other objects in an area of space. A galaxy can be thousands, millions, or billions of light-years across.

gas planets—The planets beyond Mars that are made up mostly of gas.

interstellar—In the space between the stars.

light-year—The distance a ray of light travels in one year; about six trillion miles.

meteorites—Particles of matter or small rocks that burn up in the atmosphere of a planet.

nebula—A cloud of dust and gas in space. *Nebula* comes from the Latin word for "cloud."

protoplanetary disk—An area in which a star-and-planet system may be forming.

protostar—A star that is in the process of forming.

quasar—Quasi-stellar object; a distant and tremendously bright starlike object. Quasars can be one hundred times as bright as a galaxy.

radiation—Energy given off in the form of waves or particles.

spectrograph—An instrument that separates light into a spectrum of colors.

spiral—Spinning in to a central point like a whirlpool.

supernova—Enormous explosion of a star that can be up to a million times brighter than the original star.

variable star—A star that is constantly changing its size and brightness.

FURTHER READING

Books

Cole, Michael. *Hubble Space Telescope*. Berkeley Heights, N.J.: Enslow Publishers, Inc., 1999.

Gribbin, John R. *Time and Space*. New York: DK Publishing, 1994.

Jayawardhana, Ray. *Star Factories: The Birth of Stars and Planets*. Austin, Tex.: Steck-Vaughn Company, 2001.

Oxlade, Chris. *The Mystery of Black Holes*. Des Plaines, Ill.: Heinemann Library, 2000.

Scott, Elaine, and Margaret Miller. *Adventures in Space: The Flight to Fix the Hubble*. New York: Hyperion Books for Children, 1995.

Sumner, Carolyn. *An Earthling's Guide to Deep Space*. New York: McGraw-Hill, 1999.

Vogt, Gregory L. *Spacewalks: The Ultimate Adventure in Orbit*. Berkeley Heights, N.J.: Enslow Publishers, Inc., 2000.

Internet Addresses

National Aeronautics and Space Administration. *National Space Science Data Center*. September 1, 1994. <http://nssdc.gsfc.nasa.gov/photo_gallery/photogallery.html>.

The Space Telescope Science Institute. *Highlights and Regular Features*. <http://hubblesite.org/>.

The Space Telescope Science Institute. *Images and Press Releases*. April 4, 2001. <http://oposite.stsci.edu/pubinfo/pictures.html>.

INDEX

.